A New Inquisition

A New Inquisition:
religious persecution in Britain today

Jon Gower Davies

Civitas: Institute for the Study of Civil Society
London

First Published July 2010

© Civitas 2010
55 Tufton Street
London SW1P 3QL

Civitas is a registered charity (no. 1085494)
and a company limited by guarantee, registered in
England and Wales (no. 04023541)

email: books@civitas.org.uk

ISBN 978-1-906837-15-0

Independence: Civitas: Institute for the Study of Civil Society is a registered educational charity (No. 1085494) and a company limited by guarantee (No. 04023541). Civitas is financed from a variety of private sources to avoid over-reliance on any single or small group of donors.

All publications are independently refereed. All the Institute's publications seek to further its objective of promoting the advancement of learning. The views expressed are those of the authors, not of the Institute.

Typeset by
Civitas

Printed in Great Britain by
Cromwell Press Group
Trowbridge, Wiltshire

This book is dedicated to
Ben and Sharon Vogelenzang,
two thoroughly decent human beings.

Acknowledgement

Thanks are due to David Green, two anonymous referees, Denis MacEoin, Catherine Green and Claire Daley for helping this book to happen.

Contents

Author

Jon Gower Davies retired from the University of Newcastle ten years ago. He lectured, first, in the Social Studies Department, and then in the Department of Religious Studies, of which he was Head. For 20 years he was a Labour Councillor on Newcastle City Council. He is the author and editor of books and articles on a wide range of topics, including *Bonfires on the Ice: the multicultural harrying of Britain* and *In Search of the Moderate Muslim* published by the Social Affairs Unit; and on attitudes to death and dying in the ancient religions of the world, published by Routledge. He has a particular interest in war and war memorials as definers of what he calls 'Eurochristianity'.

He was born in North Wales. From there, after the war, he went with his family to Kenya, then a British colony. He lived in Mombasa, went to school in Nairobi, and travelled widely through East Africa. After a short spell in the Kenya Regiment, a part of the British Army, he left for England to attend Oxford University. Two years in America, which included attending Brandeis University and participating in the 'Freedom Summer' in Mississippi, ended with his return to England. Since 1965, he has lived in Newcastle upon Tyne with his wife Jean. They have three children, who now have children of their own. He is a communicant member of the Church of England.

Foreword

The freedom to speak our minds without fear or favour is always high up the list of things we believe to be worth fighting for. Thinking for ourselves instead of just obeying orders is also prominent and so too is a willingness to respect authority until it over-steps the mark, when it will be met with determined defiance. Police officers tempted to be insolent or civil servants inclined to be officious tend to be reminded that they live in a nation based on law, not unfettered power. Moreover, it is law legitimised by general consent and softened by a live-and-let-live ethos.

And yet we had a law prohibiting blasphemy until 2008. It is true that the distinguished judge, Lord Denning, declared it a 'dead letter' in a 1949 speech and that the conviction of *Gay News* in 1977 served only to bring blasphemy law into ridicule.[1] The last person to be imprisoned for blasphemy was John William Gott in 1921. He was given nine months with hard labour, upheld on appeal in 1922. He died soon after his release, possibly as a result of hardships suffered in prison. His crime was to have published an anti-Christian pamphlet called *Rib Ticklers*, which among other things compared Jesus' journey into Jerusalem on a donkey with the actions of a circus clown. It was his second conviction that year. Earlier in 1921 he had been given six months with hard labour for blasphemous libel, on that occasion for publishing a book entitled *How to Prevent Pregnancy*, which was considered obscene.[2]

Such episodes show that, even in a liberal nation, every now and then minorities with a mean streak gain access to power. As this study by Jon Davies shows, we are going through one of those moments now and, yet again, the liberal majority needs to reassert the convention that the law should be used, not as a weapon to suppress unpopular opinions, but rather as the protector of free speech.

In April 2010 Harry Taylor, a militant atheist, very nearly suffered the same fate as Mr Gott. He put some leaflets mocking Christianity and Islam in a prayer room at Liverpool's John Lennon Airport. He was not charged with blasphemy but with causing religiously aggravated intentional harassment, alarm or distress under the Public Order Act. The judge sentenced him to six months in prison suspended for two years, imposed a fine of £250, and required him to carry out 100 hours of unpaid work. In addition the judge imposed an ASBO prohibiting Taylor from carrying religiously offensive material in a public place.[3] Taylor's defence was that he was merely putting his own 'rational' view. And he could be forgiven for thinking that he had a right to do so. When Parliament passed the Racial and Religious Hatred Act of 2006 clause 29J entitled 'Protection of freedom of expression' had been inserted. It said: 'Nothing in this Part shall be read or given effect in a way which prohibits or restricts discussion, criticism or expressions of antipathy, dislike, ridicule, insult or abuse of particular religions or the beliefs or practices of their adherents, or of any other belief system or the beliefs or practices of its adherents, or proselytising or urging adherents of a different religion or belief system to cease practising their religion or belief system.' Parliament had made its intentions clear but the Crown Prosecution Service (CPS) disregarded its wishes and used the looser provision of the Public Order Act as amended by the 1998 Crime and Disorder Act.

Throughout most of human history the suppression of unwelcome opinions has been the norm. One of the great triumphs of liberalism has been to separate the discovery of factual truth from the assertion of religious doctrine. Whether it is right to stand, sit, kneel or lie down during prayer can never be resolved by discussion, but whether the Sun goes round the Earth or vice versa can. Until modern times no sharp division was made between sin and holding incorrect factual beliefs. Religious authorities were the guardians of correct opinions and challenging their doctrines called into doubt their authority. Consequently they often used the full powers of the state to suppress dissent. In 1600 the Catholic Church burnt Giordano Bruno at the stake in Rome for claiming that the Earth went round the Sun and it forced Galileo to recant similar views in 1632. Open societies in which we try to settle our differences without violence have been a great human achievement and, because freedom of speech is overwhelmingly supported in Britain, we are not as alert to the risk of its overthrow as we should be.

As Jon Davies' book shows, the growth in accusations of 'hate crime' now threatens freedom of speech. Worse still, there is evidence of biased application of the law. In a recent case a Muslim man defaced a war memorial in Burton upon Trent by spraying the words 'Islam will dominate the world—Osama is on his way' and 'Kill Gordon Brown' across the plinth.[4] He was prosecuted for criminal damage, that is for neither a racially nor a religiously aggravated offence. The CPS said that the defacing of the memorial did not attach to any particular racial or religious group, despite the fact that the Burton upon Trent war memorial, like so many others, is a Christian and British memorial, carrying Christian and British symbols. And people who read the story found themselves thinking that, if a non-Muslim had defaced a Muslim building the system would have thrown the book at him. And so it was for Mr and Mrs Vogelenzang, the hotel owners who committed no crime and whose misfortunes are described by Jon Davies. As a result of a conversation with a female Muslim guest, they were accused of a religiously aggravated hate crime and pursued by the police and the Crown Prosecution Service, contrary to the evidence. When the full story came to court, it transpired that a Muslim doctor had also been eating breakfast in the hotel and found nothing objectionable about the Vogelenzang's conduct. His integrity and courage saved the day. And to speak of courage is no exaggeration. He has asked for his name to kept confidential for, amongst other things, fear of retaliation by Muslim extremists.

Some police forces and the CPS seem to be interpreting statutes in favour of members of ethnic and religious minorities and in a spirit hostile to members of the majority population, defined as 'white' or 'Christian'. It is legitimate to ask whether this trend is the result of the actions of sectarian groups within the police force and the CPS. The CPS gives official encouragement to a 'staff network' called the National

Black Crown Prosecution Association (NBCPA). Founded in 2001 the organisation was given recent official endorsement by the Director of Public Prosecutions (DPP) when he attended its AGM in October 2009. He was not the first DPP to back it. In 2005-06 it received £80,000 from the CPS and members of its executive committee were given over 300 days off to perform NBCPA duties.[5] Its main objective is to advance the careers of ethnic minorities within the CPS but it also takes an interest in the impact of CPS decisions on members of ethnic minorities. Whether this concern threatens the impartiality of the CPS is not clear. But other harmful effects of race-based policies have already led to open criticism by some CPS staff.

The atmosphere of intimidation is such that they find it necessary to remain anonymous. In February 2010 the *Sunday Times* published an account by Sameena Patel (not her real name), who reported that ethnic minorities were being given jobs within the CPS that they could not do. Often they could not even speak English properly. In one case Patel wrote that it was 'worrying when you ring someone up about a case, often a serious one, and you have trouble understanding what they are saying. Or you get skeleton arguments or documents drafted that simply make no sense and are written in pidgin English'.[6]

The activities of race and religion-based groups within the criminal justice system, including the police, the probation service and the CPS, are such that a public inquiry is now needed. This study by Jon Davies explains why it matters. Groups that act in a sectarian spirit have no place in a system whose essence should be justice and impartiality.

David G. Green

A New Inquisition: religious persecution in Britain today

Inimicitia vincit omnia

In March 2009 Mrs Erica Tazi was a guest at the Bounty House Hotel, Aintree, Liverpool. She was staying at the hotel while she was a patient on a 'pain management' course taking place at a nearby hospital. The hospital had for some years placed block bookings with the Bounty House Hotel and was indeed its main source of income. Mrs Tazi had married a Muslim and converted to Islam. On the morning in question she had come down to breakfast wearing traditional Muslim clothes. In the foyer of the hotel she had taken part in a discussion with the hotel owners, Ben and Sharon Vogelenzang, about the respective merits of her religion (Islam) and theirs (Christianity). This experience led her to make a formal complaint to the Merseyside police about what she said were offensive remarks made by the Vogelenzangs about the Muslim prophet Muhammad and her Muslim clothes. The police, advised by the Crown Prosecution Service, prosecuted the Vogelenzangs under the Public Order Acts, as amended by the 'Religious Hatred' section of the Anti-Terrorism, Crime and Security Act of 2001.

This, then, was and is a case about the new legal concept of 'religious hatred' or 'religiously aggravated hatred'.

Over several months a team of six police officers, led by a detective chief inspector, assembled a case

1

against the Vogelenzangs. Mrs Tazi was at various stages supported by the Islamic Human Rights Commission (IHRC), while the Vogelenzangs were supported by the Christian Institute, which provided them with the services of a barrister and solicitor. In December Judge Richard Clancy dismissed the case, commenting that all religions were religions of peace, but that it might be best in practice not to engage in discussions about religion: and that 'the European Union gives us all a right to religious freedom'.[1] Vogelenzang supporters cheered the verdict.

This case was the immediate cause and occasion of this essay. In spite of the verdict, it was a hackle-raising demonstration of disquieting changes in the relationship between our history, the citizen, his or her religion, his or her civil society and the state. Matters traditionally dealt with in civil society are now being held to be beyond its competence, to be seen as more properly and insistently the domain of the state—in effect, of the police and the courts or tribunals. Things change almost casually: Judge Clancy's verdict was most welcome, but when, for instance, did it come about that we owe our 'religious freedom' to the European Union and not to our historical inheritance and our Common Law? Are judges, even judges giving the 'right' verdict, so qualified in theology that they feel able to offer doctrinal guidance? Is the Crown Prosecution Service so prudent in its understanding of 'religious hatred' that it should be free, with no penalty for error, to mobilise the power and resources of the state against ordinary citizens who make ordinary comments—or indeed extraordinary comments—about this or that god or his representatives on earth?

In this country, for some centuries we have been accustomed to dealing with such matters 'amongst ourselves', so to speak: *not*, as some versions of secular liberalism would have it, 'in private', but in a public sphere regulated by our own good sense and within the framework of our historical inheritance. More and more of the day-to-day transactions of social life are currently being transferred from the voluntary self-regulating sector to the domain of state advice and state regulation, of police and 'quango' surveillance and inspection and, as in this case, of judicial regulation and decision. This takes place for the most benign of reasons: the notion of 'rights', both individual and minority rights, is the conductor of much of the transfer: and nowhere more so than when associated with efforts to eliminate the various forms of 'Hatred' and 'Discrimination' with which we are surrounded.

There are now more than 35 Acts of Parliament, 52 Statutory Instruments, 13 Codes of Practice, 3 Codes of Guidance and 16 European Commission Directives which bear on 'discrimination' and the animosities and the hatred which lie around, behind and in front of it. Together, various 'Public Order' Acts and related legislation such as the Racial and Religious Hatred Act of 2006 now make it illegal to hate anyone because of their race, colour, ethnic origin, nationality, national origin, religion, lack of religion, gender, gender identity, sexual orientation, disability, (old?) age.[2] The British Humanist Association wrote (rather appealingly) that 'it [is]

3

difficult for anyone to understand their rights and responsibilities, and there are numerous inconsistencies, with some people having more rights than others'.[3] To remedy this deplorable state of affairs, in which some people have more rights than others, Parliament passed the 'Single Equality Act' in April 2010. As far as 'equality', 'rights' and 'religion' are concerned, this promises to be a magnificently speculative venture: The Equality and Human Rights Commission (EHRC) assures us that in order to earn the Commission's protection, a religion or belief 'must be recognised as being cogent, serious, cohesive and compatible with human dignity', while another EHRC document wisely informs us that religion, unlike gender, race and disability, 'is a relatively new area of reflection'.[4] The *Sunday Times* of 7 March 2010 reports that, in the view of the EHRC, Vegans, Vegetarians and Teetotallers are to be protected by the proposed new legislation, their beliefs being 'heartfelt', unlike those of Marxists, who are not to be protected, presumably because they exemplify none of the above virtues.

This essay is about religious hatred, though this has overlaps with racial hatred and all the other hatreds. The following case exemplifies this intermixture—and the oddity of judicial attempts to regulate such things.

F—k off out of Burnley

In 2009, 23 year-old Tauriq Khalid, while driving around outside Burnley Police Station, took to making two-fingered gestures at a BNP demonstration and at its leader Mr Nicholas Griffin. Mr Khalid told Mr

Griffin to 'f---- off and get out of Burnley'. He was found innocent of the 'racially motivated' offence with which the Burnley Police charged him. Mr Khalid's actions, words and gestures seem, on the face of it, to indicate at least hostility and animosity towards Mr Griffin—and perhaps more. Mr Griffin told Preston Crown Court that Mr Khalid's activities and gestures were accompanied by 'racial remarks' ('white bastard') and also included the proffering by Mr Khalid of a hand both shaped and flourished in the manner of a pistol, threatening death. Mr Khalid denied this, describing his fingers as slanty-perpendicular and apart—a familiar two-fingered gesture—and not horizontal and united—a gun: and the court chose to believe him. From such a case, one may perhaps be forgiven for assuming that there are many forms of hatred, and that our courts (and any reasonable man or woman) will have some difficulty in identifying which of these forms are legal and which not. Mr Khalid clearly had some dislike of, or even animosity towards, Mr Griffin: rarely would anyone consider that 'two fingers' and a brusque invitation to 'f---- off out of Burnley' indicated affection: but to take a man to court for such an attitude?

Such a law-induced concern about subjective feelings and their conjectural translation into physical expression may well have unfortunate consequences: the two-fingering Mr Khalid offered no comment and left Preston Crown Court as quickly as he could.[5] The case took three days. Mr Khalid might well have been thinking that whatever feelings he had about Mr Griffin, the court had tacitly made, to his benefit perhaps, but also to his (and our) confusion, a fine and troubling distinction between the animosity-hostility (which he admitted) and the hatred (which he denied). Where this left Mr Khalid, within the beleaguered ramparts of his soul, he alone knows.

We know more, perhaps, about the general effect of the 'anti-hate' policies of the last ten years or so: hatred is certainly in the air. When, on 22 October 2009, eight million people watched the BBC's *Question Time*, it was a mass celebration (Latin *celebratus*, an event attended in great numbers) of hatred. From the beginning of the programme (and indeed from very much before the beginning of the programme), the BNP's Nick Griffin was cast in the role of the much-hated hatred: and the Chairman and the members of the BBC Panel lost no time in demonstrating how much and how liberally they hated hatred. In this, and for this, they were zealously and enthusiastically and volubly cheered on by a hatred-hating studio audience. Fortunately, as we have seen above, there is now in existence a substantial amount of legislation (Acts, Statutory Instruments, Codes of Practice etc.) which is aimed at keeping such an invigorated hatred under control.

Law and the reasonable man and woman

It is not surprising that there are some 'inconsistencies' in all this legislation. 'Hatred', one of prime movers of history, has in its own right been the major preoccupation of poets, composers, dramatists and (in our time) psychoanalysts and other more vulgar types; and in its interconnection with emotions such as envy, jealousy, bitterness, petulance, fury, malice, is both undeniably a 'fact' and yet too huge to be 'defined'. 'Religion', too, is a large and lumbering presence in practically all human societies, a source and object of ceaseless disputation, of rapture, terror, triumphalism, consolation, bigotry, illiberalism and of ineffable joy: it too has a real and forceful raw existence, a restless storm capable of being put in no constraining vessel. To add the two together, to create a justiciable and criminal offence, seems to invite such a heaping of Babel upon Babel as to lead quite legitimately to Francis Bennion's comment that such laws have abolished the traditional standard of English law, that of 'the reasonable man (and woman)'.[6] Bennion quotes Lord Macmillan:

> In the daily contacts of social and business life human beings are thrown onto, or place themselves in, an infinite variety of relations with their fellows; and the law can refer only to the standards of the reasonable man.

The story of the passage of the 'hate laws' through Parliament and, more crucially, the surrender of 'the reasonable man' to the multicultural policies and practical operational 'requirements' of the Government, the Crown Prosecution Service and the police, has resulted in some singularly worrying court cases, one of which is the occasion of this essay: The law has been invited to insert its punitive, plodding and primitive self into areas of life from which we have long been accustomed to assume not simply its absence, but the positive existence of a freely-negotiated civic culture. In this culture and civil society we accept an obligation to sort things out for ourselves—as reasonable men and reasonable women, without the benefit of a police presence and a minatory State. Such a civic culture can only too predictably cower, dwindle and grovel when faced by coercion and the assiduous bustle of the law.

The term 'hatred' appears in title and text of several pieces of criminal legislation. It is not necessarily presented as an offence in, of and on its own account, but can also be seen as something which *aggravates* ordinary public order offences, such as assaulting or stabbing someone or (less tangible) causing someone alarm and distress. These are the relatively familiar public order offences. However, when such an 'ordinary' offence is 'aggravated' by 'hatred' or 'hostility' based on race or religion, or gender, or age, then the sentence, too, is 'aggravated', i.e. increased. Hatred is, of course, not at all like a punch in the face, a stab in the stomach or the theft of your motorcar: little has to be imputed to or inferred from such actions, they have their own very evident meaning: people know when they have been punched.

It is not so easy to know when you have been hated—or, indeed, when you have yourself been hating—and for how long and to what depth and to what effect. 'Hate' becomes even more of a problem when 'religion' enters the legislative-judicial universe. It is very clear from the Parliamentary record that some legislators, at least, had a legion of scruples about intruding the law into a subject-universe which is occupied by practitioners and protagonists who are, at one and the same time, both fiercely dogmatic and generously guileless about 'religion' and loyally dismissive of its putative association with 'hatred'. In the more practical world of the police and the Crown Prosecution Service, the concept was 'operationalised' through recourse to a principle established by the Macpherson Report on the murder of Stephen Lawrence in 1993. In words which have now become part of the common language of the law, we are told that 'a racist incident is any incident which is perceived to be racist by the victim or any other person'. A CPS Hate Crime Report of 2008-2009 invokes the pedigree:

> This year is the tenth anniversary of the Stephen Lawrence, or Macpherson Report. The report was very influential across the criminal justice system and framed not only the legislation recognising racist hate crime but also the religious, homophobic and disability hate crime legislation that was to come. It shaped the fundamental changes this government has put in place to support victims and witnesses in playing their part in our criminal justice system.[7]

There is now little point in drawing attention to the very serious flaws in the Macpherson Report. This has been most definitively done by my colleague Norman Dennis[8]; but, holed, rudderless and blasted though it is, the great chugging barge that the Report became wallows on, trailing behind it the all-enveloping wash from which the criminal justice system draws its basic premise, that:

> A 'Hate Incident' is defined as: Any incident, which may or may not constitute a criminal offence, which is perceived by the victim or any other person, as being motivated by prejudice or hate.

9

A 'Hate Crime' is defined as: Any hate incident, which constitutes a criminal offence, perceived by the victim or any other person, as being motivated by prejudice or hate.[9]

This 'standard' simply 'solves' the definitional problem by ignoring it: as Humpty Dumpty said 'When *I* use a word, it means just what I choose it to mean—neither more nor less. The question is: Which is to be master, that's all'.[10] 'Hate' is what the 'victim' says it is, or what 'any other person' says it is: and it is this 'definition' which, 17 years or so after the Stephen Lawrence case, entered the world of 'religious hatred' as:

A (religious) hate crime is a criminal offence which is perceived, by the victim or any other person, to be motivated by a hostility or prejudice based on a persons religion or perceived religion.[11]

The proverbial 'Reasonable Man' may well be forgiven for asking: and what is religion, never mind a 'perceived religion'? To these long-puzzling questions, we have, in the Schedule to the 2006 Racial and Religious Act, the following Alice-in Wonderland answer:

'religious hatred [is] hatred against a group of persons defined by reference to religious belief or lack of religious belief... The reference to 'religious belief or lack of religious belief' is a broad one, and is in line with the freedom of religion guaranteed by Article 9 of the ECHR. It includes, although this list is not definitive, those religions widely recognised in this country such as Christianity, Islam, Hinduism, Judaism, Buddhism, Sikhism, Rastafarianism, Baha'ism, Zoroastrianism, and Jainism. Equally, branches or sects within a religion can be considered as religions or religious beliefs in their own rights. The offences also cover hatred directed against a group of persons defined by reference to lack of religious belief, such as Atheists and Humanists. The offences are designed to include hatred against a group where the hatred is not based on the religious beliefs of the group or even on a lack of any religious belief, but based on the fact that the group do not share the particular religious beliefs of the perpetrator.[12]

To assist the identification of hatred when its legality or illegality is under question, the Crown Prosecution Service has provided several very lengthy documents (see Notes), amongst which we find the following example of a 'hate case'.

A person used racially abusive language to a doorman when expressing anger and frustration at being denied admission to a nightclub. He was found guilty under section 28 (1) (a) of the Crime and Disorder Act 1998 (as amended by the Anti-Terrorism, Crime and Security Act of 2001). In commenting on this case the CPS insists that 'the point being made [is] that ordinarily, the use of racially (or religiously) insulting remarks would, in the normal course of events, be enough to establish a demonstration of hostility'.[13]

'Ordinarily'? 'In the normal course of events'? 'Or religiously'? 'enough to establish a demonstration of hostility'? Does such guidance clarify or merely compound confusion? Further confusion arises out of various official inclinations to define 'hatred' as 'hostility' (with little evident embarrassment at the possibility of a charge of tautology). It may well be, too, that police confusion is compounded by the difficulties of applying the rules of religious hatred to their own colleagues: what, they were asked to consider, should they make of the Muslim police woman who refused to shake hands with the Metropolitan Police Service Commissioner at her passing out parade? What rules would she be offending, if any, if she refused to shake hands with (male) members of the public?[14] The very title of this 40 page document (*ACPO GUIDANCE: Guiding Principles for the Police Service in relation to the articulation and expression of religious beliefs and their manifestation in the workplace*, 23 October 2007) shows that little clarity flows from the most prolix attempts to 'write down the rules'.

The Durham Banana

Perhaps it was this understanding of the fugitive and amorphous nature of 'hatred' which lay behind the decision of the jury at Newcastle Crown Court to acquit the then Councillor McElhone of Derwentside, County Durham. In February 2009 Councillor Iain McElhone was accused of causing racially or religiously aggravated harassment, alarm or distress.[15] He had been accused of doing a 'monkey impression' in front of and toward an Asian shop and its owner, of making monkey noises while brandishing a banana at the shop or its owner, and of scratching his armpit with the banana, like an ape. In defence, McElhone said that he had simply taken the banana out of his pocket so it didn't get squashed and that he had scratched his armpit with it because he had eczema: 'I was wearing a tight leather jacket and took [the banana] out of my pocket so it didn't get squashed. I do sometimes take fruit out with me. I had an ulcer and was advised to eat fruit. If I was scratching my armpit I must have been itchy, but I certainly wasn't making monkey noises'.[16]

Although Iain McElhone was found innocent by Newcastle Crown Court, at the time of writing he is still engaged in discussions with his employer, the County Durham and Darlington Fire and Rescue Service. This employer, *at the time of the arrest* (when McElhone must be presumed to have been innocent), and well before Mr McElhone's acquittal (after which he was indubitably innocent), felt both able and obliged to produce a public statement, saying that 'We will not tolerate any racist behaviour by our staff. We cannot comment on any matter relating to an ongoing police investigation. The fire and rescue service will be conducting its own investigation into this matter'.[17] The relations between Mr McElhone and his employer are, at the time of writing, still unresolved. The legal case cost thousands of pounds.

The case which elicited the writing of this pamphlet is that of Sharon and Ben Vogelenzang, the owners and managers of the Bounty House Hotel in Aintree. As we have seen above, at breakfast time in early March 2009, in the dining room and foyer of the hotel, Ben and Sharon Vogelenzang had taken part in a conversation about religion, and had, it was later alleged, commented to a female Muslim guest that in their opinion Muhammad was a 'war-lord' and the various styles of female Muslim dress were a 'form of bondage'. The guest, Mrs Erica Tazi had allegedly given as her opinion the (conventional) Muslim belief that Christ was not the Son of God but merely a (minor) prophet; she claimed that in describing Muhammad as a 'war-lord' the Vogelenzangs had gone so far as to liken Muhammad to Hitler. Consequent upon this theological-political

13

discussion, the actual initiation of which was one of the points at issue, Mrs Tazi complained to the police. The police interviewed and charged the Vogelenzangs with a religiously-aggravated public order offence, under the Public Order Act of 1986 and the Crime and Disorder Act of 1998, as amended by the Anti-Terrorism Crime and Security Act of 2001. On the news of the pending case, that is at a time when, by long-established practice, the Vogelenzangs must be regarded as innocent, the local NHS authority cancelled their bookings, thus, via a public presumption of culpability, adding the prospect of bankruptcy to the couples' troubles. District Judge Richard Clancy rejected the CPS's case, thus enabling the Vogelenzangs to avoid a fine of £5,000 and the acquisition of a criminal record, which would have certainly wrecked both their reputation and their business. Indeed, at the time of writing, and after the 'not guilty' verdict, the hospital block-bookings which provided 80 per cent of the Bounty House income, have not been renewed: and the Vogelenzangs will in all probability be driven out of business. This may be compared to Ian McElhone's suspension by his employer well before the court hearing which, in the event, found him innocent. This legislation spreads its suppuration well beyond the formal confines of the law.

Non culpa sed ignominia

While the Vogelenzang case was proceeding through the police/CPS/court system, the Vogelenzangs were the recipients of threats and hate mail, and described themselves as 'living a nightmare… drained emotionally and financially'.[18] They could not see why the police had been so enthusiastic in pursuing them. The Christian Institute both provided the money for the defence of the Vogelenzangs and organised supportive prayer meetings and a demonstration outside Liverpool Magistrates Court. The declaration of innocence by District Judge Clancy did not stop the vilification to which the Vogelenzangs were subjected. To the Islamic Human Rights Commission, which had supported Mrs Tazi throughout the trial, the acquittal of the Vogelezangs proved that 'Mr and Mrs Vogelenzang acted out of hatred which is a reflection of the anti-Muslim sentiment in popular discourse', that they had 'subjected [Mrs Tazi] to intense abuse', and that as a consequence of the acquittal 'Muslims will further lose faith in the system'.[19] It is hard to believe that a different verdict would have altered the views of the IHRC. In another response to the verdict, Barry Duke, the editor of *the freethinker* (*'the voice of atheism since 1881'*) described the Vogelenzangs as 'two rude nutters... a daft pair of Christian fundamentalists who run what appeared to be a Basil Fawlty-type establishment in Liverpool'.[20] In his Editorial, Barry Duke wrote that 'to be *Vogelenzangstered* would mean that you'd been subjected to a tirade of faith-based abuse' of the kind he himself had got used to in his 'long years as a militant atheist'. Barry Duke's Editorial drew heavily on a piece in the *Sunday Times*[21] by Rod Liddle: and it was perhaps Duke's atheistic zeal which led him to miss much of the irony in Liddle's article. Liddle, true to his liberal form, insisted that the case gave us in microcosm 'everything that is hideous about

Britain... spite, pettiness and self-righteousness, the po-faced and now institutionalised political correctness, the magnificent lack of common sense'. Liddle asked 'By what process did this fairly mild, if unpleasant spat end up before a magistrate with the proceedings—which stretched across two days with barristers and the like—paid for by you and me?' This is a perfectly correct understanding. Yet within the impeccably liberal attitudes of Liddle, complemented by the 'militantly atheistic' views of Barry Duke, there were to be found some of the perhaps unintended consequences of the 'hatred' legislation, in that its very exercise seems to create the very atmosphere it was designed to prevent. Neither Liddle nor Duke had been to the trial, nor had they met the Vogelenzangs: yet they felt free to describe the real victims of this trial (Ben and Sharon Vogelenzang) as 'two rude nutters' (Duke) and as 'treating their guests... in the manner of self-righteous and pig-ignorant Christian bigots' (Liddle). From where do such attitudes come? What promotes and facilitates this desire to heap humiliation on two people, found innocent, whose way of life and business have been destroyed? Where in all of this, for example, can we find such comments applied to Mrs Tazi?

To be fair, Duke and Liddle very explicitly regarded the hate laws as stupid ('fabulously inane'), but their personal abuse of the Vogelenzangs is so typical of the debasement of a public debate about religion which until recently was carried on without the intervention of the police and the inevitable conjuring-up of media-yelping and authentically hate-driven abuse. A friend of mine, a gay Anglican vicar, clearly reacting to the role of the Christian Institute in the defence of the Vogelenzangs (he sees the Christian Institute as being anti-gay) took the view that it was very foolish for hotel workers in the service sector to initiate religious debate in their own hotel. He hummed some kind of agreement when I suggested that the Vogelenzangs could, as business people, be assumed to be well aware of that.

If the critics of the Vogelenzangs had attended the trial, they would have heard being read out to the court a letter from a Muslim doctor who had been a guest at the Bounty Hotel, who had nothing but praise for the Vogelenzangs: 'I am a Muslim and I know they are devout Christians but... I have never found them to be at all judgemental. They were as friendly with me as with any other guest... Should I need to [stay in Liverpool again] I would not hesitate in again stopping at the Bounty House Hotel.' The doctor (who has asked not to be identified here) had left the hotel for the hospital before Mrs Tazi, but he felt able to say that 'the atmosphere was not at all awkward' (Mrs Tazi claimed that she was being harangued) and that 'if there were any offensive remarks I would have recalled these, as I, being a Muslim myself, would have been offended if anybody mocked my beliefs'.[22] Judge Clancy seemed to think (there was no record taken of his summing-up) that the prosecution had not proved its case that the Vogelenzangs had initiated the discussion about the respective merits of Christianity and Islam, or that they had been intemperate, or any more intemperate than Mrs Tazi, in the articulation of their views. The Judge expressed the court's sympathy for the inordinate delay between the initial interviews by the police and the date on which the Vogelenzangs were actually charged and brought to trial. He also offered a theological opinion, which he was no doubt qualified to make, that all religions were religions of love.

The judge may well have been sympathetic: yet it does not alter the fact that two very decent people were humiliated, distressed and nearly bankrupted by the court appearance and by the prolonged period of police inquiry and the attendant publicity. The hate laws are criminal laws operating under the police and the CPS; and their parading of assorted 'miscreants' through the degradation ceremonies of the courts, will create more abuse and hatred—as we have seen in the comments of the Islamic Human Rights Commission and Barry Duke. Little attention will be paid to the quiet demurrals of the likes of the doctor, who was also a guest at the hotel. In this, there is a peculiar conjunction of two very different, indeed antithetical aspects of contemporary culture: First, a long-incubated tradition of British secularism and atheism, with its well-developed combative and caustic hostility to religion and to its adherents—well expressed here by Duke and Liddle: and, secondly, there is an equally combative Islam, as dour as any Covenanter, and well represented here by the IHRC, determined to press its religious claims and to protect its followers. Separately, these two forces have been major subscribers to the dominant 'multicultural' politics of the last decades: and they seem on occasion, as in this case, to make common cause. Such a perverse alliance carries within itself the seeds of nothing but further conflict.

The hate laws, trundled through the courts by the CPS and the police, will create more hate, and related humiliations. Pushed into the narrow boundaries and purposes of the law, 'hatred' will transform its alleged perpetrators into quasi-secular sinners and abject anxious penitents, rendered mute, confessing them-selves (on the surface anyway) to be in need of punishment and forgiveness, conferred compulsorily if necessary. The alleged sufferers from 'hatred' will be assured that they are deemed, by those in authority, to be gentle victims only too available for 'rescue' by the busily helpful and well-intentioned zealots of the state. These laws will weigh most heavily on very ordinary men and women:

> Should I sigh because I see
> Laws like spiders webs to be?
> Lesser flies are quickly ta'en
> While the great break out again.[23]

This deeply divisive activity by the state will be flawed in part because the energy behind the hate laws, the head of steam stoked up by these laws in the CPS and the police, is powerful but uncertain in its direction and purpose: or, to be blunter, it will be biased. Not all religious encounters are subject to such state intervention as were the Vogelenzangs. At about the same time as Mr Khalid, Mr McElone and the Vogelenzangs were enmeshed in the nets of the hate laws, the Dutch MP Geert Wilders made, at the second attempt (having been earlier banned) a visit to London. On 16 October 2009 he was greeted by so vehement and threatening a demonstration by some Muslims that (in spite of a large police presence) he was asked to change his route to the Parliament building so as to avoid having to pass near the gathering of Muslims—one of whom indeed, via television cameras, challenged Wilders to get the police to withdraw and to approach them when, we were told, 'within two minutes' he (Wilders) would sharp learn the error of his ways (*not*, very definitely *not*, said the Muslim man, that he himself would do such a thing, unspecified). The police line stood face to face with, and only yards apart from, the Muslim demonstrators, actively doing nothing. Some hint of what Mr Wilders might expect could be found in the words of a couple of the Muslim demonstrators, who shouted that:

> The punishment in Islam for insulting the prophet is capital punishment… He should take a lesson from Theo van Gogh who took the punishment… We are here to teach this dog a lesson… His bark is at the heart of every Government in Europe, in the heart of every unbeliever, wherever this dog hides there will be a Muslim. Islam will dominate, will conquer England and Holland and the European crusaders will be destroyed. Muslims are everywhere. Israel will be destroyed. Who ever insults the prophets there is only one punishment—Kill him! They are all hypocrites they prosecute Muslims for hatred but not Wilders. We will take this no more. If this was a Muslim State his head would be on a stake! They are killing Muslims everywhere. Wilders is running scared let him come out there to meet the Muslims without the police protection he will in two minutes see his punishment. There is only one punishment. Islam will enter every heart some will be elevated some downtrodden. Those people who insult Islam are under constant protection, they don't live a life. They should learn from that.[24]

Mr Wilders changed the route to his venue (though not, one assumes, his message). No arrests were made. Indeed, the Muslim Council of Britain (MCB), apparently unaware of the anti-Wilders 'demonstration', objected to 'the rapturous welcome [Wilders] is receiving in the name of free speech'.[25] Hate was perhaps too obvious to be recognised by the MCB? Or too 'multicultural' to be policed? There are, it would appear, different kinds of 'hate'.

The hate laws are clearly not, and were perhaps not intended to be, random in their operation. The latest Hate Crime Report from the CPS, in which unfortunately racial and religiously aggravated crimes are not disaggregated, has the CPS claiming to have 'set the bar for constant improvement in performance'.[26] By this, the CPS clearly means that they seek an *increase* in the number of cases brought and in the number of convictions achieved: the CPS was concerned with the 'enduring reasons for unsuccessful outcomes'. The total number of such crimes (racial, religious) actually fell from 13,201 in 2006-7 to 11,845 in 2008-9. The Merseyside force, which initiated the prosecution against the Vogelenangs, had the 'worst' record, with a conviction rate of 73 per cent (all forces: 82 per cent), and a concomitant 'unsuccessful' (i.e. 'not guilty' or not taken to prosecution) rate of 27 per cent (all forces: 18 per cent). The CPS Report for 2006-2007, which did disaggregate data for cases of religious hate, stated that of the relatively few cases reported by police forces in England and Wales (27), the majority (63 per cent) had Muslims as the victim. The Report for 2008-9 (again, not disag-

21

gregating racist and religious hate crime) stated that the majority of the defendants were White British males.[27]

Hate and multiculture

> The attempt to ensure that every type of person, belief, habit and preference is included equally in all important settings requires comprehensive measures that continuously counteract the way people naturally view and deal with each other… Everyone is required to participate enthusiastically in a never-ending and all-embracing campaign for inclusiveness and against that acceptance of the reality of human differences which is now called *hatred.*[28]

> Heads will be forced to list children as young as five on school 'hate registers' over everyday playground insults.[29]

The Macpherson Report, and its quasi-masochistic adoption by the police, provided the legitimation for what is now the received wisdom in these matters, that a hate crime or hate incident occurs when the 'victim or any other person' has a perception that he or she is the victim of prejudice or hate. Further, and drinking more deeply in the waters of 'institutional racism' (the other main nostrum of the Macpherson Report), all police forces (and indeed all citizens) are to assume themselves to be 'racist' until there is proof to the contrary. In the case of the police and the CPS, such proof can be most obviously located in a very visible and virtuous zeal in the detection and prosecution of those who 'hate'. The operational definition, 17 years after Macpherson, is repeated in 2010:

> A (religious) hate crime is a criminal offence which is perceived, by the victim or any other person, to be motivated

by a hostility or prejudice based on a persons religion or perceived religion.[30]

In the most general sense, the ubiquitous and augmenting hate laws are a product of the officially-promoted and officially-sanctioned multiculturalism of the last 30-40 years: they were unknown before then, as was multiculturalism. Britain was, until the 1960s, an amiably (but resolutely) monocultural only-recently-democratic nation-state. In the 1960s, driven by multi-cultural ideologies, purposes and programmes, new-style ruling elites in British politics, government and media set themselves the task of promoting global Equality in the face of (and often in the teeth of) nation-state Democracy: Democracy had, in the view of these elites, rather let Equality down, necessitating, insistently and progressively, 'affirmative action' or 'positive discrimination' in several fields. This process attained its fullest political expression under the Blair and Brown Labour Governments, governments of professional politicians almost completely disconnected from the traditional hierarchical bases of political life. The process found its quintessential institutional expression in the Equality and Human Rights Commission; its demo-graphic expression in the settlement (legally or other-wise) in Britain of several millions of people from very different countries; its cultural expression in the saporous house-style of the BBC; and an intellectual respectability in the steady transformation of British University-based social studies from its customary preoccupation with class and poverty to the more lucrative field of race and ethnicity.

'Poverty' was perhaps the bridging concept here, as many new arrivals could be shown to be less well-off than many of the indigenes (though very much better off than the non-migrators who had stayed at home). Great rolling fog-banks of political correctness descended upon our political, governmental and educational institutions. If, within this new multicultural world, anyone ventured even mild individual gestures or grimaces of discomfort or disagreement, then they increasingly found themselves addressed and advised by well-meaning (and well paid) persons concerned to persuade them of their errors and, if necessary, to force them to be free of them. Only as the first decade of the twenty-first century came to an end did certain small mutterings from Democracy, and after certain revelations of official ambitions,[31] did it begin to dawn on the saints who had gone marching in with multiculturalism that they had gone, perhaps, too far ahead of those, their fellow-countrymen, who were not happy with what was going on. Even here, the zealots for Equality were able to dismiss their opponents by classifying them as the disgruntled remnants of the 'old working class', implicitly presented as 'racist'. Survey after survey showed that, to the contrary, the majority of the British people, including many thousands of the 'Black and Minority Ethnics', found themselves out of sympathy with the ruthlessly egalitarian ambitions of their liberal rulers.

Hate and religion – and Muslims

The suicide bombings in London on 7 July 2005 were the first incidents of religious warfare in England since the end of the

24

seventeenth century and are a terrifying development which would have been dismissed as impossible only 30 years ago.[32]

The quote from Neil Addison, above, introduces a particularly Muslim variant of multiculturalism. Islam is, or Muslims are, the wave-makers, the mould-breakers, the trend-setters of multiculturalism—though it is extremely doubtful (one hopes) that less volatile adherents like Hindus, Sikhs, Jews or Zoroastrians will too keenly follow the paths so vigorously blazed. The new Islamic presence in Britain grew up under the aegis of, and was legitimated by, the initial multi-culturalism and achieved (along with other multi-cultural religions and cultural practices) a level of tolerance and licence unique in the history of this or any other country. Islam, thus (though temporarily) camouflaged as merely one aspect of multiculturalism, then developed—as Addison's quote indicates—along rather angrier lines to the extent that it is (in more ways than one) *the* major author of the hate laws. In November 2001 the House of Commons debated the proposed 'religious hatred' sections of the Anti-terrorism, Crime and Security Bill. Sir Patrick Cormack put it to the Home Secretary that:

> because of the reaction in Muslim countries to the dreadful events of 11 September, and because of the fear among many Muslims that subsequent actions would be seen as a war against Islam, he was persuaded to introduce measures to our domestic law.[33]

Mr Blunkett indicated that this was indeed one of the reasons.

25

The Commons had earlier been made aware—as if they needed to be after the attacks on the World Trade Centre—that the problem with Muslims and Islam was not just another multicultural story: Mr Frank Dobson, for example, told the MPs that the 'racist thugs' of the BNP were putting it to other Asian groups that 'You Hindus and Sikhs ought to gang up with us and beat up the Muslims'.[34] It is difficult to believe that the BNP's approach to Sikhs and Hindus got them very far, whatever hostility there might be between the three Asian cultures. These evident ethno-religious differences were in part related to the fact that Sikhs (but not so obviously or easily Hindus) were 'protected' (like Jews) by laws about *racial* hatred, whereas Muslims, not being a race, were not. Muslims had, or were, *a religion*: and a religion, like all religions truly believed, with 'form'. As Christopher Caldwell puts it:

> If you measure Islam by the intensity of its followers convictions, by its importance in political debates, by the privileges it enjoys under the laws of many European countries, or by its capacity to intimidate potential detractors, then Islam is not the second religion of Europe, but its first.[35]

Muslims, as Sir Patrick Cormack pointed out (above), had 'entered' the House of Commons through their faith's apparent association with the murder of over 3,000 people in New York: indeed, the 2001 Anti-Terrorism, Crime and Security Act, on which Sir Patrick was speaking, was a response to just that attack. It was the murderous suicide attacks of 9/11 and 7/7 that 're-branded' immigrants from South Asia: for example, 'Pakistanis' became 'Muslims', thus evoking the Parliamentary efforts to regulate expressions of religious (rather than racial) difference and dis-agreement. Part Five of the 2001 Act included major changes in the sphere of 'religious hatred', but a year or so later, before the murders on the London Underground and on a London bus, the Muslim Council of Britain, writing to the House of Lords Select Committee on Religious Offences, wrote:

> We should like the Select Committee to take due account of the incontrovertible evidence… that Muslims in the United Kingdom feel particularly vulnerable, insecure, alienated, threatened, intimidated, marginalized, discriminated and vilified since the September 11 tragedy.[36]

Immediately following this, and clearly in an effort to pre-empt a muttered 'well what do you expect', the MCB asked the House of Lords to consider 'most carefully [and] with due weight the Runnymede Trust on Islamophobia' which was issued 'prior to September 11'.[37]

It is impossible to understand the atmosphere in which police, prosecutors and courts work within the hate laws without understanding the precise nature and outcome of Muslim self-presentation and self-exculpation. There is a clear pattern here. The standard initial Muslim institutional response to things like 9/11 or 7/7, or the more recent expressions of Muslim aggression like the murders in Mumbai or the killings of US soldiers by a fellow-soldier at an army camp in Texas, is to make a radical dis-association of themselves and 'real' Islam from their co-religionist killers. Then there follows the 're-recruitment' of the spectre of the violence so as to make it, as it were, a counter-poise against whose weight they pile up another series of favourable and exonerating self-descriptions and a bundle of pleas or demands for exceptional treatment, indulgence and special privilege. All this is energetically articulated as a defence against the (real or anticipated) 'unfair' and 'unjust' response of the non-Muslim majority society to the (totally a-typical and unrepresentative) Muslim extremists and killers. In this way, the majority non-Muslim or indigenous society is denied the chance of seeing *itself* as the 'victim' in this story: and Muslim organisations such as the MCB can depict *themselves* and their irrefutably 'non-violent' 'Moderate Muslim' community as the *real* victim, a victim, that is, not of their 'own' violence (an extrinsic embarrassment, to be cast adrift) but also of the consequent waves of (quite unjustified) 'islamophobia' (*sic*) emanating from the non-Muslim society. Through such rhetoric, we are persuaded that we should sympathise with Muslims for *their* victim-hood, and proceed to defend them with as much of the gentle busy-ness of the law as an inherently decent and liberal society can mobilise. This self-depiction of Muslim communities embattled in the West was well-articulated by the Muslim Directory for 2007/8.[38] The Directory's 'Publisher's Note' starts by saying 'Though we had hoped that we would be able to write a more 'up-beat' note from the last edition, the events that have taken place since have worried both us and the community'. It continues:

> The community has always upheld the rule of law and will always denounce the warped individuals whose aim it is to hurt the whole of our society. We have been living in peace

here for over 100 years and will continue to do so but recent events have ensured that Islam itself is now a target of institutions and individuals from all walks of life including the media and government.

The brief and dismissive reference to terrorism (arms-lengthed off as 'warped individuals') is immediately capped by the complaint about the way in which the community ('living in peace for 100 years') is now being targeted. This provides the overture for a long paragraph which follows, which, as a list of the assaults and injustices being visited upon the Muslim community may be taken as a version of what British civil society and the police look like to these influential Muslims. We learn of:

The continued stereotyping of Islam and its adherents; the incarceration and proposed extradition of British citizens to the USA including Babar Ahmad without any recourse to the British courts; the politicisation of public institutions, such as the police; the shooting and arrest of innocent Muslims; the arrest of Muslims whose '*sub judice*' case details are actively leaked by the police with the alleged involvement of the Home Office; the media 'frenzy' which is allegedly 'stoked up' by our government to side-track local and global issues; the release, without charge, of many of those arrested without the same scale of media reporting; the increase in Islamophobia and the refusal of public institutions such as the Metropolitan Police to acknowledge this; the active government withdrawal from liaising and consulting with main-stream Muslim organisations; the ridiculous and continued blame, demand and onus on the whole community by the government for it to 'prevent terrorism' and yet at the same time actively alienating large quarters of the community; the systematic curtailment of our civil liberties; the arrest, imprisonment and solitary confinement of people for several years without charge in the UK and the obliteration of '*habeas corpus ad subjiciendum*' and continued torture and in-humane detention of hundreds in Guantanamo; the extradition of individual Muslims to countries of torture and our governments compliance with the USA on rendition; the continuous demands led by our 'free and unbiased' media to ban and censor non-violent political organisations and some charities and criminalise certain opinions and the demand on the community to distance themselves from oppressed people around the world have greatly affected, concerned and worried us as British Muslims and what effects this will have on the future of our children in this country.

Keep off kept off

An alien world indeed—and one probably unfamiliar to most British non-Muslims, i.e. to most of us native Brits. However 'warped' or 'not-really-Muslim' Muslim terrorists might be, they and their adamant and voluble co-religionists (as above) have effectively carved out for their religion an immunity to serious criticism. Thus, for example, in an almost casual way, in reviewing a book by Osama bin Laden's wife, Robert Harris wrote that the two humorous writers Dick Clement and Ian La Frenais 'sadly abandoned' an idea of a comedy series (about bin Laden settling down with his family in an ordinary English suburb) because of the 'chances of causing grave offence'.[39] 'Sadly abandoned!?' Chickened out, surely!? And in a very destructive way! The making of jokes and the cultural exchanges facilitated by humour are both civilised and civilising; and their suppression has the opposite effect. What we cannot, in cheerful safety, laugh at, and what we cannot, in a law-free way, swap as humour, will steadily become a repressed and muttering buried cache of hostility, resentment and animosity. The suppression of jokes (or cartoons) in any public discussion about religion is a feature of the last twenty years, a consequence of angry and occasionally violent Muslim reaction to what Muslims regard as blasphemous.

The bold and brave of the Arts world also let us down. We have British artists like Grayson Perry who like many of the freedom-loving foot-soldiers of the Arts establishment, is happy to trash Christianity but who avoids Islam 'because I feel real fear that someone will slit my throat'.[40] As we know, Perry is not the only prudent artist or author. Nick Cohen describes a media that is scared, since the Rushdie affair, of offending Muslims and scared, too, of offending the multicultural establishment. This, writes Cohen, produces a dominant media culture happy to insult, in its various popular television dramas, Hindus, Jews and Eco-Greens—but not Islam.[41] Christians, of course, are fair game—and used to it, confident in their ability to cope: no Christian demanded either the suppression of the Life of Brian or offered violence to the producers of the film.

So the violence, although rejected by both the dominant media managers and by 'official' Muslimhood, has worked. The antiphonic 'appeal', made to our better British natures, on behalf of a self-described 'beleaguered' and 'moderate' Muslim minority 'community', has also worked—the main concern is now with 'the victim' (the moderate Muslim) and not too much with any of their critics. While, with some difficulty, our Security Services maintain an anxious watch upon terrorists, a variety of Government-sponsored schemes see many millions of pounds spent on Government programmes like PREVENT,[42] regarded by the Home Office as funding 'local authorities, police and partners to stop the spread of violent extremism'. And then there is the Department for Communities and Local Government's 'Faith Communities Capacity Building Fund' and the 'Community Leadership Fund', not to mention general grants for 'Preventing Violent Extremism', aimed specifically at local authorities with a Muslim population of five per cent and over. Inevitably, there have been accusations of waste and misdirection, of money going to organisations which, while moderate themselves, do nothing to 'tackle extremism', and even of money going directly to organisations perhaps closer to 'extremism' than they should be. As counter to this, Muslim organisations such as the MCB (which, together with its numerous affiliates, received nearly £1 million.), have accused the Security Services of infiltrating the PREVENT schemes, i.e. of spying on ordinary Muslims in 'the biggest spying programme in modern times'. The MCB urged the Government to 'move away from Cold War mentalities and to realise that British Muslims are part of the solution, not the problem'.[43] Earlier, the MCB had welcomed Cohesion Minister Shahid Malik's assurance that in future the PREVENT agenda would avoid focusing on 'some local communities and particularly Muslim com-munities', and would instead 'cover extremism emanating from all quarters'.[44] The MCB had the BNP in mind. It had its own community in mind when, in March 2010, it hosted a 'closed-meeting (*sic*) of distinguished Parliamentarians, academics, journalists, police, public servants, and community represent- atives' to discuss 'Tackling Islamophobia and Reducing Street Violence Against British Muslims': the participants endorsed calls for an 'All-Party Parlia- mentary Committee on Islamophobia'.[45] Earlier that year the MCB had announced its participation in the POWER2010 Campaign which calls for a decen- tralisation of political power, through such devices as directly elected mayors and a recall or removal of MPs through constituency referenda.[46] *At every level*, there- fore, of our national life we will see, if the MCB has its way, an effective Muslim presence in (amongst many other things) the matter of the operation and implementation of the hate laws and the deployment and operational practices of the police. The MCB may well have had, as do other Muslim organisations, concern about the surprisingly high levels of criminality amongst Muslims who live in Britain. For an extended treatment of this see my *In Search of the Moderate Muslim*.[47] Suffice it here to say that the Muslim community, at about two per cent of the general population, provides about nine or ten per cent of the prison population. Over and above questions of 'extremism', Muslims have, or are, a particular communal problem as far as the police and the criminal justice system is concerned.[48]

Community community community

The promiscuous deployment of the (generally meaningless) word 'community' is also part of the campaign against hate. Racial and religious crimes are committed, the CPS tells us, not just against individuals but against whole 'communities': the following quotes are from the CPS document *'Guidance on prosecuting cases of racist and religious crime'*:[49]

> The CPS refers to hate crimes as having 'serious… real and lasting effects on individuals, communities and the whole of society'.[50] The CPS has a vision of 'increasing the confidence of black and minority ethnic communities, as well as increasing year on year the satisfaction of victims and witnesses, whilst respecting the rights of defendants'.[51] 'We have consulted people from black and minority ethnic communities and faith communities and taken their comments into account in writing our policy and guidance.[52] 'The confusion, fear and lack of safety felt by individuals have a ripple effect in the wider community of their racial or religious group. Communities can feel victimised and vulnerable to attack'.[53]
>
> 'When people hate each other because of race, such hatred may become manifest in the commission of crimes motivated by hate, or in abuse, discrimination or prejudice. Such reactions will vary from person to person, but all hatred has a detrimental effect on both individual victims and society, and this is a relevant factor to take into account when considering whether a prosecution is appropriate'.[54] Put simply, the CPS seeks in these ways to demonstrate its 'commitment to promoting race equality in accordance with our obligations as a public authority under [various Acts]'.[55]

A parallel CPS document, *The Prosecutors' Pledge*,[56] asserts that:

> The Pledge is a further step toward putting the objective of placing victims at the heart of the criminal justice system and is applicable to all prosecuting authorities… Where appropriate, the prosecutor will also take into account the

likely effect the type of crime you have suffered may have on your local community.

Community! Policing and the burden of proof

While 'the defendant' appears from time to time in these and other documents, their vocabulary ('community', 'victim') stems primarily from the conventional decencies of multiculturalism: *Community, Community, Community*. One can only wonder what effect this kind of mission statement has on, for example, the police. In an only slightly different 'hate' context, Lord Waddington said:

Police officers, pressurised by diversity training, seem duty bound to come down like a ton of bricks on people who express disagreement with the behaviour of some gay rights activists, and members of the public are left feeling harassed and frightened.[57]

Lord Waddington was in no sense encouraging 'gay bashing', but was supporting the age-old rights of (in this case) Christians to make their long-held views known on this (and any other?) subject. Lord Waddington would not perhaps be reassured by suggestions that this 'inter-communal' problem could be solved by giving various minority communities (Muslims and Sikhs) their 'own' police.[58] Metropolitan Police Chairman Peter Smyth said 'It's political correctness gone mad. We are talking about the creation of a separate force within a force'. Parbinder Singh of the Metropolitan Police Sikh Association disagreed, saying that 'a white officer is [never] going to be fully conversant with a Sikh'.[59] In October 2009 Peter Smyth's point was perhaps made when a

National Association of Muslim Police (NAMP) Press Release issued some 'Advise (*sic*) to Muslim Community', urging young people to resist the temptation to 'misbehave' in response to 'so-called protests' by 'Racist Far Right groups'. The NAMP said that while 'the police will act to deal with disorder no matter who carries it out, we do not want young people to be arrested'. It is clear to which 'young people' they were referring.

The triumph of victims

Not only have the forces of the state developed a sympathy, or perhaps empathy with minorities (and against hate) which have a quite distinct political agenda: so too have we seen demolished some of the traditional defences of the citizen. Under various sections of the Equality Act of 2006, claims of religious discrimination must be brought to the County Court; and, somewhat surprisingly, under section 68 of the Act, the County Court could make any order which the High Court could make. Moreover, under section 66(5) the 'burden of proof' is reversed:

> In proceedings under this section, if the claimant (or pursuer) proves facts from which the court could conclude, in the absence of a reasonable alternative explanation, that an act which is unlawful by virtue of this Part has been committed, the court shall assume that the act was unlawful unless the respondent (or defender) proves that it was not.[60]

With a police force already force-fed and enervated by the dubious diet of the Macpherson report, and a CPS already so diligently impressed with the need to suppress religious hatred, who can doubt the way in which such legal prescriptions and invitations will take them? Communal love and moral virtue can be assumed to attach to those police forces and those prosecuting bold radicals who seek and attain the official 'targets' set by the hate campaign.

Citizen's arrest – the untrusted unreasonable citizen

Further, in pursuit of hate, they will be well assisted by the fact that in the hate legislation, yet another centuries-old right has been removed. In the Parliamentary debates and voting about the draft Racial and Religious Hatred Act of 2006, the Government actually lost major sections of the legislation—but succeeded in removing, from all treatment of such offences, the right of citizen's arrest. An 'Explanatory Note' gives some indication as to why the Government found this necessary. In its concern to operationalise 'hatred', the Note first of all offers the standard list of 'religions widely recognised in this country such as Christianity, Islam, Hinduism, Judaism, Buddhism, Sikhism, Rastafarianism, Baha'ism, Zoroastrianism and Jainism' and goes on to say:

> Branches or sects within a religion can be considered religions or religious belief in their own right. The offences also cover hatred directed against a group of persons defined by reference to a lack of religious belief, such as Atheists and Humanists. The offences are designed to include hatred against a group where the hatred is not based on the religious beliefs of the group or even on a lack of any religious belief, but based on the fact that group do not share the particular religious belief of the perpetrator.[61]

Aware, perhaps, of the invitation to sectarian warfare offered by such ideas, the 2006 Act included a section removing from the scope of the legislation the centuries-old general right of citizen's arrest. In the Commons, Home Office Minister Paul Goggins (a Roman Catholic Christian Socialist) said that otherwise 'individuals could try to use the power of citizen's arrest inappropriately and perhaps maliciously'. Why religious people should *in general* be held to be more prone to 'maliciousness' than their secular fellows, is unclear to me: but Mr Goggins felt that since the police would undoubtedly be 'cautious' in invoking the Act, so 'we [MPs] should also be cautious about the powers we might give ordinary citizens'.[62] Note that Mr Goggins seemed to think that the right to citizen's arrest was something that he could 'give'! Perhaps Mr Goggins was led to assume, by the evident murderous bigotries of the London bombings, that all people, when moved or confronted by religion, would become malicious—or worse. This is like the old prohibition on the scriptures in the vernacular—the people cannot be trusted with religion, hated or loved, abhorred or venerated, so render them powerless by rendering them speechless.

However, as we have seen with PREVENT, and as another way of getting 'communal' involvement in the religious hatred business, 'ordinary citizens' were invited back into the hunt for hatred by the creation (in theory within a year of the Act coming into force) of 'Hate Scrutiny Panels', a device promoted by the CPS, local Police Authorities and Local Councils, and Community Involvement Panels—all to be in place by

March 2008. These Panels and their associated Community Involvement Panels had some kind of precedent in the various 'Muslim Safety Forums' which appeared in the mid-2000s.[63] The CPS sees such 'Hate Scrutiny Panels' as involving 'people from diverse backgrounds including people from groups concerned with challenging racist and religious discrimination'.[64]

The Charities Act 2006

A further downgrading of the majority or natal religion of this country is to be found in the 2006 Charities Act. There are of course considerable fiscal benefits in charitable status. The Act removed from the various local and national administrative institutions of the Church of England (and other Christian churches) the presumption that, in advancing religion, education and the relief of poverty, they were acting 'charitably', i.e. for the public benefit. This presumption, which had evolved over centuries, was protected and regulated (lightly) through Parliamentary Statutory Instrument: the regulation was 'light' because the nation's Parliament was familiar with the nation's institutions. The Act did away with all this, and, in lieu of Parliamentary over-sight, and the presumption of public benefit, required the Church, along with all other charities, to satisfy the administrative requirements and rules of employees of the Charity Commission. This means that all 13,000 Parochial Church Councils, many of the Finance Committees of the 43 Dioceses, the Archbishops' Council, the Church Commissioners and the countless host of charitable organisations in whole or in part related to the Church must now satisfy Ms Susie Leather's Charity Commission that they are of public benefit. To carry this very substantial task forward, the Charity Commission established a Faith and Social Cohesion Unit, which saw as its first task an analysis of the organisational competence and financial probity of mosques and related Muslim charities. To assist in the task of ascertaining the qualification for charitable status of these mosques, the Charity Commission hired BMG Research, an organisation based in Birmingham. Their Report of February 2009[65] states that out of 716 organisations, contact, i.e. telephone contact, was made with 247 (34 per cent), 'an encouraging response rate', said the authors. Telephone contact was the sole method of contact, and involved a pre-prepared 'prompt list' of questions. The Charity Commission may well have better data on which to base its rational-bureaucratic decisions: it is hard to believe that such data bear much comparison with the cumulative evidence for, and the cultural weight of centuries of Church-related charitable activity.

The blasphemy laws

> Life and meaning lie in the escape from determinate being, in transition to something other than what one already is— the less definable the better. Like sex, drugs, ambition and violence, change and diversity are this-worldly substitutes for transcendence. Anything, even change for the worse, is better than here-and-now reality and the requirements imposed by a specific community and way of life.[66]

For several centuries Christianity in Great Britain, and in particular the Anglican version of it, was protected by the 'blasphemy laws'. In 2008 these laws were, as part of the post 9/11 and 7/7 accommodation with Islam, removed. Most of my friends, including some of those in my (Anglican) Church, thought this was right and proper. Half of my friends think that from a purely liberal perspective there is no justification for a law which protects one religion *only*. The other half thinks that from a purely secular perspective there is no justification for *any* law protecting *any* religion. All of my friends think that a law which has fallen into disuse is a law which brings 'the law' into disrepute, and is thus deserving of repeal.

These objections to the blasphemy laws have been made for many years by many people. It cannot be too forcefully asserted that the blasphemy laws have *not* been abolished *as a result* of these arguments and objections. Abolition has had to wait for the era and pressures of multiculturalism, especially of Islam. This was both cause and occasion for the abolition of the blasphemy laws, just as it was for the debasement of the 'burden of proof' and for the removal of the citizen's right of arrest. Thus we have the strange world-view of the ex-Bishop of Oxford when he asked: 'in the light of the widespread outrage at the conviction of the British teacher for blasphemy in the Sudan over the name of a teddybear (*sic*) is it not time to repeal our own blasphemy law?'.[67] Did the Bishop see, in the existence of the British blasphemy laws, some kind of 'parity' between the UK and the Sudan, when in the Sudan the 'offence' against its laws produced a trial, the threat of the lash, actual imprisonment—and general mayhem and death-threats on the streets of

Khartoum, whereas in England the last attempt to use the blasphemy laws produced little but yawns and indifference in all but a tiny section of hippiedom and luvviedom—and almost no response when the laws disappeared? Does he expect that the removal of offences against 'the formularies of the Church of England' will see joy and contentment break out all over the Muslim world when more Danish cartoons appear? Has the fatwa against Rushdie now been lifted? Are the Sudanese now at peace with Teddy Bears called Mohammad? Furthermore, ex-Bishop Harries was profoundly mistaken in thinking that the removal of the ancient and (narrow) blasphemy laws would result in an end to the realm of blasphemy: in fact, the realm now stretches wider still and wider, defined and policed by laws for which he argued and voted: and it protects at least one religion which has already shown itself to be remarkably out of tune with our secular culture and religious stance.

The 2008 Criminal Justice and Immigration Act, in which blasphemy was 'abolished', followed the 2006 Racial and Religious Hatred Act (itself an amendment to the Public Order Act (c.64)) which, in creating the criminal offence of 'Hatred against persons on religious grounds', provided some sort of 'defence' for *all* religions. This was indeed its purpose! An Explanatory Note to the 2006 Act claims that 'The Act will ensure that the criminal law protects all groups of people defined by their religious beliefs or lack of religious belief from having religious hatred intentionally stirred up against them'.[68]

However eloquent the distinctions made in Parliament between (in effect) 'hatred and 'blasphemy', the new laws do not simply remove blasphemy but extend it: and (again, in effect) extend it to provide a special *de facto* protection to Islam: CPS figures quoted above demonstrate this very clearly.

In such a context, and in spite of the strongly-held opinions of my friends, I can see several grounds for regret at the passing of our old blasphemy laws. In their very narrowness and non-use is to be found some justification for their retention. In Durkheim's teaching that law is made manifest in and by the public and painful humiliation of a real live criminal, we can find the corollary, i.e. that such punishment (or rather the lack of it) is also a way of making manifest those areas of our social life which law does *not* regulate. An unused law makes a point in a way in which, post abolition, its simple non-existence will not. It acts as a signpost to our *actual* history, of how we *in fact* treat problems once highly and popularly regulated (primarily because seen as destructive of the public peace), but now rendered tractable and amiable by the very experience of life under regulation, an experience leading, now, to the non-exercise of the power of the law. The experience—not shared by those religions under which 'heresy' and 'apostasy' are currently matters of life and death—is signified by the existence of our blasphemy law in all its unused glory: it is the British civic culture around the law which provided the lesson: which is why the Bishop of Oxford's semi-rhetorical question was and is so silly.

43

Context is all

'When critiquing other religions, Christians must seek to be winsome'.[69]

The actual words are 'Christians should not be afraid to continue to exercise their role in the public square and to proclaim Christian Truth, which may involve critiquing other religions. We must seek to be winsome and to appeal to others in doing this'.

'A (religious) hate crime is a criminal offence which is perceived, by the victim or any other person, to be motivated by a hostility or prejudice based on a person's religion or perceived religion'.[70]

Nothing in this Part shall be read or given effect in a way which prohibits or restricts discussion, criticism or expressions of antipathy, dislike, ridicule, insult or abuse of particular religions or the beliefs or practices of their adherents, or of any other belief system or the beliefs or practices of its adherents, or proselytising or urging adherents of a different religion or belief system to cease practicing their religion or belief system.[71]

While, in the schools of theology, purist exegetes insist that 'there is nothing but the text', in post-9/11, post 7/7 multicultural Britain there is 'nothing but context'. How else to explain the extraordinary use of the word 'winsome'? Being 'winsome' would not be much of a guide between the hard rocks in which *anyone* can shout that they are being hated (see the second quote above) and the soft and seductive place in which you are assured of the right to ridicule and insult other religions (the third quote). In the most recent case (on-going at the time of writing), again involving Liverpool, 'militant atheist' Harry Taylor will probably find little solace in S 29J of the 2006 Act.[72]

He has been charged with religiously aggravated harassment because he left anti-religious leaflets in a room used for worship at Liverpool's John Lennon airport. The leaflets were as scatological about Christianity as about Islam—as scatological, said Harry Taylor, as Lennon himself: but Nicky Lees, the airport chaplain, felt herself to be 'deeply offended and insulted'. The police were called. In court, prosecuting lawyer Neville Biddle, being no doubt an experienced and qualified theologian, said that while freedom of speech was 'one of the most important rights we have [and] it must be jealously guarded', finished by saying that such 'a right was not without some prescription'.[73] 'Preposterous', said Mr Taylor. He faces a possible prison sentence.

The repealing of the old blasphemy laws, and their replacement by a very different kind of law, should be seen not simply as an enhancement of equality and freedom, a move to winsomeness, but as yet another concession to more profoundly inegalitarian and restrictive religious cultures—*reculer pour mieux tomber*, perhaps. As is so often the case, the discussions about repeal focused on or invoked Islam as a vocal, demanding or importunate presence which has to be propitiated—how often do we hear Sikhs or Hindus insisting on concessions aimed at removing the 'privileges' of the Church of England?[74] How often do we hear Anglican bishops expressing concern about the 'sensitivities' of Sikhs or Hindus? The current public conversation about religion and the state is dominated, *sotto voce* or otherwise, by an intention to 'protect' religion, especially the religion of newly

45

arrived minorities, and amongst them, particularly of those minorities adhering to Islam. This is a reversal of several hundred years of the British way of 'having' or 'doing' religion.

A public conversation

> Nothing is required for... enlightenment except *freedom*; and the freedom in question is the least harmful of all, namely, the freedom to use reason *publicly* in all matter... The *public* use of one's reason must always be free, and it alone can bring about enlightenment among mankind... The vocation for free *thinking*... gradually reacts on a people's mentality (whereby they become increasingly able to *act freely*), and it finally even influences the principles of *government*, which finds that it can profit by treating men, *who are now no more than machines*, in accord with their dignity.[75]

Over many centuries, and in our country through the work and lives of exemplary men such as Wycliffe, Tyndale, Cranmer, and James the First's 'companies' of translators, a scripture available in the vernacular slowly, painfully and precariously built the possibility of a publicly debateable and publicly debated religion. Protestants hanged and quartered Catholics, and Catholics in turn burned Protestants—until slowly (very very slowly) we all learned that there were better ways of 'doing religion'—or even of doing without it. There were, and still are, very considerable regional or 'national' variations in this story, Wales, Scotland and Ireland making their own distinctive contributions. Generally, though, in this process the domain of coercion and of state interference was slowly and steadily modified and diminished, while the domain of

46

the argumentative public was enlarged. In this public domain, and in particular in the 'long nineteenth century' (1832-1932), religion and its many secular critics and opponents carried on a long and vigorous argument. In the city in which I live (Newcastle upon Tyne) the major monument commemorates the century between the passing of the Great Reform Bill (1832) and its centenary (1932), when a new inscription was added referring to the 100 years as 'a century of civil peace'. This is, as a moment's rumination would confirm, a truly remarkable claim for the evolution of our civic culture.

The contours and contrarieties of this very long process are ill-understood if seen as the construction of a 'private' or 'privatised' religion. It was 'private', perhaps, in that our society was slowly, unevenly and at considerable cost freed from the compulsions and supervisions of the state, but not 'private' in that it disappeared into the secret, unrecorded and restricted vocabularies of the home. 'Personal' is a better word than 'private'. In both the nineteenth and twentieth centuries, arguments about religion and atheism were taken very personally indeed. No one reading the literature of England could possibly think that 'religion' was discussed only in the bosom of the family, or that it was discussed in isolation from its secular interlocutor. It was a public, often quarrelsome but eventually (or 'until recently'?) civilised affair, symbolising the transformation of religion from a mystery known only to the few and conferred or imposed upon the many, to a cultured and considerate form of conversation between the citizens of an

47

increasingly liberal and free society, with an increasing respect for both secular and atheist views. In the century or so which followed the Great Reform Act of 1832, religion—in this country, Christianity—was a major topic of public conversation, a conversation which can be seen expressed not only in our literature, but in the lapidary texts of our architecture, our public buildings, civic memorials, street names, war memorials, in our calendar, our system of public holidays, our great cemeteries and crematoria, our national and local public rituals—and in a hundred other ways, including secular and libertarian movements, demands for social and sexual liberty, in secular universities, in novels, art-works, music and modes of dress and address— and in ribald jokes and provocative scurrilities. The fact that the blasphemy law was invoked but twice in this century, and only once by the state, shows how successfully this free and jubilant conversation established itself. It is the very strength and adaptability of *this* monoculture, this inheritance, which (ironically enough) made multiculture possible. *Pace* Nietzsche, it was not God that died but dogma.

This slowly-established and never-finished project has degenerated into the kind of spectacle in which the Merseyside Police, urged on by the CPS, the ACPO and the Government, spent several months (and thousands of pounds) constructing a case of a public-order offence, aggravated by religious-hatred, against two Christian hoteliers from Aintree, Liverpool. The police, the CPS, the ACPO and the Government—the collective promoters of the law and of the case—lost. However, this did not result in a re-think of the entire business: Nicky Inskip of the CPS said that 'In considering the public interest factors in favour of a prosecution, we took into account the impact that the incident had on the victim'.[76] No doubt. Ms Inskip will, one hopes, have on her list of victims the two people who suffered most: Ben and Sharon Vogelenzang.

Non culpa sed ignominia

> To implement such a (liberal) program of social trans-
> formation an extensive system of controls over social life has
> grown up, sometimes public and sometimes formally
> private, that appeals for its justification to expertise, equity,
> safety, security and the need to modify social attitudes and
> relationships in order to eliminate discrimination and
> intolerance.[77]

Through a change in the 'burden of proof', through the removal of the right to citizen's arrest, through the erosion of the culture which rendered the blasphemy laws mute, through a belittlement of our tradition of religious charity, through the 're-education' of an already-demoralised police, and through the slow but steady increase in the ambitions and activities of the bureaucratic and prosecuting authorities of the central state, we are being advised or told to abridge the scope of the once-broad range of public conversation about religion and its various antitheses. Under the admon-itory tutelage of an augmenting band of Orwellian Hate-officials, perversely if unconsciously allied to the more-readily partisan zealots of Islam, it becomes 'wise' to 'be careful', to restrict the compass of what we say about what we believe, or do not believe, or about what others believe or do not or should not believe, and to turn what were once vigorous public conversations into a frightened, if safe, if amiable and fundamentally humourless chat about small and dwindling things. That crucial way of crossing the cultural divide, the mutual telling of scatological jokes, has now to be abandoned. In this way, our traditional public debates about religion and its critics are being made impossible. Religious multiculturalism has persuaded the majority of the people of this country that they have a serious moral flaw—that they are a majority! Further, *per contra*, we are now invited or instructed to believe that the minorities now living here have, *qua* minority, moral virtue: and that they and their concerns take political, moral and religious precedence. In the strangest of ways, the recent Labour Government set about forcing us to be free from our base emotions, especially the emotion of *'hate'*, and to inculcate in its place the sense of *shame*, shame that is about, and in particular, our religious inheritance and the values and codes of public conduct which were its progenitor, co-creator and partner in the construction of our national life. We are engaged in a liberal lower-case very British cultural revolution. Ben and Sharon Vogelenzang, whose case initiated this pamphlet and with which it comes to conclusion, are to be considered as the British equivalent of those unfortunate Chinese who were forced, in public, and with little prospect of forgiveness or rehabilitation, to confess the 'sins' they did not know they had in front the wagging minatory finger of the government-sponsored multicultural accuser. Ben and Sharon 'won' their case: but they were shamed by the very fact of having to fight it:

'the defence was not really recognised by the law, but only tolerated... The intention was to eliminate the defence as far as possible, the whole onus was to be placed on the accused'.[78] For the best part of a year, the Vogelenzangs sat in their home which was also their business, while the agencies of the state sought to bring about their humiliation: Kafka's K had the same problem:

> What days lay ahead of him? Would he find a path that would finally lead through all of this to a happy ending? While his trial was rolling on, while the court officials were sitting in the attic poring over the documents of his trial, was he expected to conduct bank [*read hotel*] business? Did that not resemble a form of torture which, sanctioned by the court, was connected with the case, and an integral part of it?[79]

This was a *trial* about *religion*: last seen centuries ago! The British people might be forgiven for thinking that their basic religious-cultural inheritance, the culture under which we have grown up, is not just out of control but under some insidious attack. This British culture validates a *public seeking* for religious truth, *not* a trial: and it is more or less at ease with jokes and ribaldries, and ill at ease with censorship of them or with threats made at their authors: what British Christian would call for a writ to put an end to the Life of Brian or issue threats to intimidate its authors? The Vogelenzangs were taken to court partly because they were accused of calling the Muslim prophet Mohammed a warlord. Visitors to Istanbul's Topkapi Palace can see the Prophet's swords, his bow and arrow, and one of his teeth allegedly damaged at the

Battle of Badr: but even if we ignore the fact that as a warrior and military leader Muhammad is lauded by Muslim tradition, and even if we should have known that he was in fact, we gather, a man dedicated, all his life, to peace—what is wrong with being wrong? We in Britain have grown up believing that the only offence in being wrong lies in maintaining an error in the face of its evident correction; and that the way to correction is via debate, not the courts; and that the suppression of debate (especially religious debate) by the agencies of the state leads not to decent civil harmony but to vexatious hypocrisies and suppressed but very real hostility. Being forbidden to express opinion, whether by actual punishment or the threat of it, or by the experience of being threatened, results, as the Psalmist has it, in a society in which 'we bless with our mouth, but inwardly we curse'.[80]

There is no need for Muslim demonstrators to invite upon 'offenders' such as the Vogelenzangs the fate of Theo van Gogh: he, being dead, can be assumed to be safely unrepentant and beyond the reach of those who hate him. Ben and Sharon Vogelenzang, now 'officially' innocent, are alive and struggling to restore their hotel business and their peace of mind. Innocent though they are, and innocent indeed well beyond the capacity of a mere court so to find them, they will no doubt recover from their ordeal—but, in their publicised humiliation and shame, they will never again venture, whether within the dining room of their modest hotel or on a Bootle bus, either defence of their own religion or critical comment on another. Keep quiet, keep silent, jest not: the recent Labour

Government has abolished the possibility of religion, of both its serious public profession and of its cheerful public execration. We have been trivialised.

Notes

Foreword

1   http://news.bbc.co.uk/onthisday/hi/dates/stories
     /july/11/newsid_2499000/2499721.stm. The editor was fined
     and given a suspended prison sentence of nine months.

2   Royle, E., 'Gott, John William (1866–1922)', *Oxford Dictionary
     of National Biography*, Oxford University Press, 2004;
     doi:10.1093/ref:odnb/47693.

3   http://www.liverpoolecho.co.uk/liverpool-news/local-
     news/2010/04/24/militant-atheist-harry-taylor-hit-with-asbo-
     for-offensive-images-in-john-lennon-airport-100252-
     26307049/;
     http://www.independent.co.uk/news/uk/crime/atheist-given-
     asbo-for-leaflets-mocking-jesus-1952985.html

4   http://www.telegraph.co.uk/news/uknews/crime/7657600/
     Muslim-walks-free-as-court-told-Osama-bin-Laden-graffiti-
     not-religiously-motivated.html

5   HMCPSI, *Equalities Driving Justice: Report On The Thematic
     Review Of Equality And Diversity In Employment Practice In The
     Crown Prosecution Service*, 2006, p. 14.

6   http://www.timesonline.co.uk/
     tol/news/politics/article7043985.ece

A New Inquisition: religious persecution in Britain today

1   *Daily Mail*, 10 December 2009.

2   Crown Prosecution Service, Fact Sheet: *Hate Crime: What is
     Hate Crime?*;
     www.cps.gov.uk/news/fact_sheets/hate_crime

3   BHA: Single Equality Act. Accessed 10 November 2009;
     www.humanism.org.uk/campaigns/equality/single-
     equality-act

4   EHRC, *What is a Religion?*. Accessed 8 March 2010;
www.equalityhumanrights.com/your-rights/religion-and-belief/what-is-a-religion/
and EHRC, *Research Report 48*, endpaper. Accessed 8 March 2010.

5   *BBC News*, 4 December 2009.

6   Bennion, F.A.R., *Doc. No: 2006.003, 170 JP*, 21 January 2006;
www.francisbennion.com

7   CPS, *Hate Crime Report*, 2008-2009, p. 7.

8   Dennis, N., *Racist Murder and Pressure Group Politics: the Macpherson Report and the Police*, London: Civitas, 2000.

9   ACPO and Home Office Police Standards Unit, *Hate Crime: Delivering a Quality Service*, 2005.

10   Carroll, L., *Alice's Adventures in Wonderland*, London: Purnell, 1975, p. 173.

11   HM Government, *Hate Crime: the Cross-Government Action Plan*, 2 February 2010, Title Page.

12   Maer, L., *Standard Note SN/PC/03768*, House of Commons Library, 10 June 2008, p. 3.

13   CPS, *Guidance on prosecuting cases of racist and religious crime*, London, p. 7;
www.cps.gov.uk/publications/prosecution/rrpbcrpol.html

14   ACPO, *GUIDANCE: Guiding Principles for the Police Service in relation to the articulation and expression of religious beliefs and their manifestation in the workplace*, 23 October 2007, p. 33.

15   *Newcastle Evening Chronicle*, 21 February 2009.

16   *Newcastle Evening Chronicle*, 23 October 2009.

17   *Newcastle Evening Chronicle*, 23 October 2009.

18   *Telegraph*, 12 December 2009.

19 IHRC Press Release, 9 December 2009.

20 *The freethinker*, vol. 130, no.1, January 2009.

21 *Sunday Times,* 13 December 2009.

22 Witness Statement, Liverpool Magistrates Court, 9/10 December 2009.

23 Braithwaite, R., Barnbe's Journal, c. 1640.

24 National Review On Line, 18 October 2009; http://corner.nationalreview.com/post?q=MTE4NTA4N2M2 MDM3M2Y1ZD12YjA1

25 MCB Press Release, 16 October 2009.

26 CPS, *Hate Crime Report*, 2008-2009, p. 7.

27 CPS, *Hate Crime Report*, 2008-2009, p. 3

28 Kalb, J., *The Tyranny of Liberalism, understanding and overcoming administered freedom, inquisitorial tolerance and equality by command*, Wilmington, Delaware: ISI books, 2008, p. 65 and p. 67.

29 *Daily Mail,* 4 March 2010.

30 HM Government, *Hate Crime: the Cross-Government Action Plan*, 2 February 2010, Title Page.

31 Neather, A., and Marrin, M., *The Sunday Times,* 1 November 2009 and Walters, S., *Mail on Sunday* 25 October 2009.

32 Addison, N., *Religious Discrimination and Hatred Law*, Routledge-Cavendish, 2007: xxiii. p. 148.

33 www.theyworkforyou.com/debates/?id=2001-11-26.673.2

34 www.theyworkforyou.com/debates/?id=2001-11-26.673.2

35 Caldwell, C., *Reflections on the Revolution in Europe: Immigration, Islam and the West*, Allen Lane: Penguin Books, 2009, p. 142.

36 The MCB to the HoLSC on the Religious Offences Bill, 7 July 2002.

37 The MCB to the HoLSC on the Religious Offences Bill, 7 July 2002.

38 *The Muslim Directory*, London, 2007/08.

39 *The Sunday Times*, 15 November 2009.

40 *Islamist Watch*, 15 November 2009.

41 Cohen, N., 'Spooked by Islamists', *Standpoint*, January 2010, p. 75.

42 3 June 2008; http://www.idea.gov.uk/idk/core/page.do?pageId=7946870

43 MCB Press Release, *Spying on Communities Contravenes Cherished British Freedoms*, 18 October 2009.

44 MCB Press Release, *MCB Welcomes the Refocusing of our Collective Responsibility in the Pursuit to Prevent Terrorism*, 12 August 2009.

45 MCB News, *MCB brings Experts and Parliamentarians Together to Discuss Islamophobia*, 5 March 2010; http://www.mcb.org.uk/article_detail.php?article=announcement-862

46 MCB, *Vote Now to Transform UK Politics: A Real Voice for the Community: Last Chance to Have Your Say*, 22 February 2010.

47 Gower Davies, J., *In Search of the Moderate Muslim*, London: The Social Affairs Unit, 2009, pp. 91-109.

48 For example see *The Sunday Times*, 16 November 2009, and Gower Davies, *In Search of the Moderate Muslim*, 2009.

49 CPS, *Guidance on Prosecuting Cases of Racist and Religious Crime*, 21 October 2005, p. 7. Accessed 8 October 2009;

www.cps.gov.uk/publications/prosecution/rrpbcrpol.h
tml

50 CPS, *Guidance on Prosecuting Cases of Racist and Religious Crime*, 21 October 2005, p. 3.

51 CPS, *Guidance on Prosecuting Cases of Racist and Religious Crime,* 21 October 2005, pp. 2-3.

52 CPS, *Guidance on Prosecuting Cases of Racist and Religious Crime*, 21 October 2005, p. 4.

53 CPS, *Guidance on Prosecuting Cases of Racist and Religious Crime*, 21 October 2005, p. 4.

54 CPS, *Guidance on Prosecuting Cases of Racist and Religious Crime*, 21 October 2005, p. 9.

55 CPS, *Guidance on Prosecuting Cases of Racist and Religious Crime*, 21 October 2005, p. 3.

56 CPS, *The Prosecutors' Pledge,* 21 October 2005.

57 *Daily Telegraph,* 16 November 2009.

58 *BBC News,* 22 July 2009 and *Sunday Express* 26 July 2009.

59 *BBC News,* 22 July 2009 and *Sunday Express* 26 July 2009.

60 See Addison, *Religious Discrimination and Hatred Law*, p. 57.

61 Explanatory Notes to Racial and Religious Act 2006; http://www.opsi.gov.uk/acts/acts2006/en/ukpgaen_20060001 _en_1; and Addison, *Religious Discrimination and Hatred Law*, p. 148.

62 Maer, L., *The Racial and Religious Hatred Act 2006, Standard Note SN/PC/03768*, Parliament and Constitution Centre, 10 June 2008, pp. 7-8.

63 See Gower Davies, J., *In Search of the Moderate Muslim*, London: The Social Affairs Unit, 2009, 103ff.

[64] CPS, *Guidance on Prosecuting Cases of Racist and Religious Crime*, 21 October 2005, p. 37.

[65] Coleman, L., *Survey of Mosques in England and Wales*, BMG Research, Project 7126, February 2009.

[66] Kalb, J., *The Tyranny of Liberalism, understanding and overcoming administered freedom, inquisitorial tolerance and equality by command*, Wilmington, Delaware: ISI books, 2008, p. 74.

[67] Maer, L., *The Abolition of the Blasphemy Offence*, SN/PC/04597, 2 May 2008, p. 7.

[68] Accessed on 9 October 2009; http://www.opsi.gov.uk/acts/acts2006/en/ukpgaen_20060001_en_1

[69] CCFON and Christian Legal Centre, *Freedom to Evangelise and Freedom of Speech,*, http://www.ccfon.org. downloaded 22 February 2010, p. 3.

[70] HM Government, *Hate Crime: the Cross-Government Action Plane*, 2 February 2010, Title Page.

[71] The Racial and Religious Hatred Act, 2006, S 29J.

[72] The Racial and Religious Hatred Act, 2006, S 29J.

[73] *Daily Telegraph* , 3 March 2010.

[74] In an earlier book, *Bonfires on the Ice*, I discussed the (unsuccessful) attempt made by Professor Tariq Modood to persuade Hindus, Sikhs, Jews and others to support the disestablishment of the Church of England. Gower Davies, J., *Bonfires on the Ice: the multicultural harrying of Britain*, London: Social Affairs Unit, 2007, pp. 92-93.

[75] Kant, I., 'What is Enlightenment?', 1784, in *Perpetual Peace and Other Essay*, translated by Humphrey, T., Indianapolis: Hackett Publishing Company, 1983, p. 42 and p. 46.

NOTES

www.christian.org.uk/news/judge-finds-couple-who-criticised-islam-innocent/, 19 December 2009.

[77] Kalb, *The Tyranny of Liberalism*, 2008, p. 6.

[78] Kafka, F., *The Trial (Modern Voices)*, London: the Hesperus Press, 2005, pp. 102-03.

[79] Kafka, *The Trial (Modern Voices)*, pp. 102-03,

[80] Psalm 62 (slightly amended).